SEASONS IN TH...
The first paperba...
loved poet.... R...
hardcover have s...

" ... he composes poetry as hymns to love ... he reacts and responds to people simply and in a way that makes most men wish they weren't so inarticulately pen-tied when it comes to writing what they feel."
—Michael Iachetta, *New York Daily News*

"He is a consummate storyteller, delivering his own material with ingratiating warmth and polish."
—Stanley Eichelbaum,
San Francisco Examiner

" ... he has a deep, probing concern about human relationships. This comes out in everything he does."
—Kimmis Hendrick,
Christian Science Monitor

" ... more than occasionally he is capable of rendering awareness into perceptions of small but haunting truths ... with the tincture of a fine irony."
—Robert Kirsch, *Los Angeles Times*

SEASONS IN THE SUN is an original *Pocket Book* edition.

ROD McKUEN

SEASONS IN THE SUN

PUBLISHED BY POCKET BOOKS NEW YORK

SEASONS IN THE SUN

POCKET BOOK edition published May, 1974

This original POCKET BOOK edition is printed from brand-new
plates made from newly set, clear, easy-to-read type.
POCKET BOOK editions are published by
POCKET BOOKS,
a division of Simon & Schuster, Inc.,
A GULF+WESTERN COMPANY
630 Fifth Avenue,
New York, N.Y. 10020.
Trademarks registered in the United States
and other countries.

ISBN: 0-671-80640-8.

Cover and design by Hy Fujita.

Cover photograph by Hy Fujita.
Photography by Hy Fujita, Rod McKuen,
Gene Palumbo, and Donald Bradburn.

Coordinated for POCKET BOOKS by Jonathon Brodman.
Printed in the U.S.A.

This is a book for E.

I've saved some sunlight
if you should ever need
a place away from darkness
where your mind can feed.

— *I've Saved the Summer*

Books by Rod McKuen

Poetry
And Autumn Came
Stanyan Street & Other Sorrows
Listen to the Warm
Lonesome Cities
In Someone's Shadow
Caught in the Quiet
Fields of Wonder
And to Each Season
Come to Me in Silence
Moment to Moment
Beyond the Boardwalk

Collected Poems
Twelve Years of Christmas
With Love . . .
The Carols of Christmas
Seasons in the Sun
Alone

Collected Lyrics
New Ballads
Pastorale
The Songs of Rod McKuen
Grand Tour

Song Books
The Annotated Rod McKuen Song Book

Author's Acknowledgement

In addition to the sources listed on the copyright page of this book, I've had the inspiration of many American poets, songwriters and singers: Lee Hays and the Weavers, whose music made me want to sing before I knew how. I owe much to Johnny Mercer, Lorenz Hart, Whitman, Mancini, Copland, Ives, Sandburg, William Carlos Williams. Singers of all kinds: Jo Stafford, Billie Holiday, Peggy Lee, Pete Seeger, Phyllis Curtin, Marilyn Horne, Mary Travers, Joe Williams, and, of course, Sinatra. Nan Talese, the first editor I ever had (who came almost too late), and my current editor, Jonathan Dolger.

Jacques Brel has not only inspired my work, but my living and life style as well. He uses the same words to describe my relationship to him and his work. I consider that the highest possible compliment.

All of these poems spring from fact as I know it—though how dull life would be without a little fiction.

Author's Note

Every year I've tried to make the summer stretch a little longer. I come to Mexico in January and February to write—always assured I'll find the sun. My concerts in the fall are planned in countries like Australia to catch the places and people as their summer begins. At home in California, I'm at the beach or stretched out in the backyard the first day of March and the last sunshiny hour of October.

The sections in this book stretch over an eight-month period. Eight or nine months of summer is the very least I promise myself a year. I like to work in the sun, play in the sun, make love in it and waste time in the sun. Though I am aware by doing so I miss the subtleties of the seasons, the colors of Vermont Septembers, the surprises of Nebraska Springs, all my life I've chased the sun.

Seasons in the Sun began as a short story. My first. Unpublished, it concerns a man who is dying and recounts his life figuratively and actually as one where all the highlights took place within some sunshiny time.

More than a dozen years ago, I brought home from France an album containing Jacques Brel's *Le Moribond* (the dying man). Although the song had nothing to do with the sun, per se, it seemed to me that Jacques' lyric—though in another language—talked about the man in my story, so I began to fuse his lyric with my short story and what emerged was an Anglo-American song entitled *Seasons in the Sun.* The title now seems like a good one for a collection of sun poems.

I have talked lengthily about my collaborations with Brel elsewhere, and in a forthcoming book on his life. Each of us has in common a sense of being loners though we have both taken the sea and the sun as mistresses, if not wives.

This collection of poems has many sources—a dozen books, stanzas from nineteen songs, new poetry, and always the sun, threading it's way through the individual works. Both the poems and the songs were written over a twenty-year span, beginning with *And Autumn Came,* published in 1954, and including a selection from *Moment to Moment* to be published in September of 1974, plus the aforementioned new material and poems written through the years that have remained unpublished till now.

When someone asks me how long it took to write a particular poem I ask what year it was published, and even if I used up only twenty minutes to commit the words to paper I add the life I've lived to the point of publication, and give that as my answer.

My poems of ten years ago are different from the ones I write today. The work I do tomorrow will be miles apart from that done yesterday. My seasons in the sun ahead are not as many as they could be. Nonetheless, they will be lived out fully—as full as I know how to make them.

Rod McKuen
Tres Vidas, Mexico
February, 1974

Contents

13

JUNE

JULY

AUGUST

SEPTEMBER

OCTOBER

Publisher's Note

The author wishes it to be known that the verses that begin and end each chapter of this book are lyrics from songs and are not to be considered poems in themselves. They include *I've Saved the Summer, Something More, Chasing the Sun, Love Let Me Not Hunger, I'll Catch the Sun, Sommerset, Kelly and Me, The Summertime of Days, Summer Moonlight, When Summer Ends, Three, Blessings in Shades of Green, Gone with the Cowboys, Love's Been Good to Me, The Ivy That Clings to the Wall, Dandelion Days, The Voyeur* and of course the title song, *Seasons in the Sun*.

SEASONS
IN THE SUN

We had joy, we had fun
we had seasons in the sun
but the wine and the song
like the seasons have all gone.

We had joy, we had fun
we had seasons in the sun
but the song and the rhyme
were just seasons out of time.

All our lives we had fun
we had seasons in the sun
but the stars we could reach
were just starfish on the beach.

—Excerpted from the song,
"Seasons in the Sun"
Lyrics by Rod McKuen
Music by Jacques Brel
English Lyric © by Rod McKuen
Published by E.B. Marks

march

for Jack Albright

And the fine sun of fifty
saw him dying and alone.
Just a man struck down suddenly
by something not yet known.
Just a man who spent all his life
hoping once to soar.
And all the while expecting
something more.
                    —*Something More*

The Pause, Before the Going
for Pam Burns

If I thought
that I was dying,
and I am
      of inattention,
           indifference
           and the need
to prove just once
      I've lived—
for someone
      other than myself,
what would/should
my reaction be?
Especially if I knew
that finally and forever
there would be no one.

Could I,
would I go back,
retrace, relive,
          remake my life,
try to prove my time
within this cage—
my body—worthwhile?

I doubt it.
What a thankless task
a waste of time
an added heartbreak
pulling all the bad times out
          would be.

But if I could sum up
all the sun times
afternoons and mornings too
I'd do it in a minute,
for I've known sun
      in blacked out rooms
behind the kind of curtain
no solar sun
    could once
        go through.

Sure as I've seen stars
I've seen the sun
     at midnight,
been warmed
    by suntanned backs
      all day
when even rain
failed to penetrate
banks and walls
of clouds outside,
sunshine people
made it through to me.

Far from my undoing
the sun has been my savior
and I'll go happy
if I can look back
one more time
at all the suns I know
          and knew.

Taking the Time

Taking time to love
is what it's all about—
what makes the clocks turn
and the sunsets come
true and without
        complication.

That doesn't mean
lying close
        in shut-up rooms
or staying always
        face to face.

It's meant to cover walking,
being apart and knowing
that coming back together
makes small distances
        even smaller.

And taking the time
            to love
is, most of all,
        caring enough
to not hold on too tightly
and yet not run too loose.

Rome Itself

I carry
down between my legs
      Rome itself,
for you love Rome
and I would drive Rome into you
or drive you into Rome.

This room your coliseum
till you board your plane.
These arms your forum,
      cats included.

Self propelled am I
between the morning
and the midnight
I glide along your groin
and earn my wings
by testing out your thighs
like some new willful
                    Wiley Post.

My flight is not away
not to or from.
Above you below you—
I soar around you and perch
upon your second pillow.

I have no need
for such mechanical devices
as winged shoes or wings.
I am made uncommon
by the need to know you
and thereby come
to know myself.

Rome
though in the distance
is no farther than the dresser
and not so far away
that I can't take you there.

For me the Spanish Steps
are centered on your tongue
and Caesar
could content himself
with California wine
had he your eyes to follow
and your breath to capture
with his own breath.

We'll go to Rome
as slowly as you like
and be there by tonight.

Moth

Awakening
this morning
after the first night
     of being loved
I heard a disillusioned moth
flapping at the windowglass
trying to reach
     the morning sunlight.

And the sun,
long fingers of it,
came through the window
picking out the dust
     in special corners.

In the pre-dawn hours
         lying together
all arms and legs and breathing
with the rain not so far away
and morning coming too soon
I hoped never to see
        the sun again.
         And now
your face and the sun
have made this room
with only ceiling sky
and avenues of sunlit dust
beautiful.

Twenty-Three

I am
and I am not
a kind man
when it comes to loving.

Help me up
if I fall down
and prop my head
against the sink
if need be.

I am sick of sunshine
when you lie
in bed
beside me.
But when you venture
through the door
I need the daylight
　　　　desperately.

Pushing the Clouds Away

Clouds are not
the cheeks of angels
      you know
they're only clouds.
      Friendly sometimes,
but you can never be sure.
If I had longer arms
I'd push the clouds away
or make them hang
   above the water
      somewhere else,
but I'm just a man
who needs and wants,
mostly things he'll never have.
Looking for that thing
that's hardest to find—
      himself.

I've been going
a long time now
along the way
I've learned some things.
You have to make
the good times yourself
take the little times
and make them into big times
and save the times
that are allright
for the ones
that aren't so good.

I've never been able
        to push the clouds away
                by myself.
            Help me.

Please.

The Meaning of Gifts

Before befriending
                butterflies
you have to meet
with midnight moths.
Perspective comes when poles
are far enough apart
to have horizons at both ends.

So trampling through the night
                        together
lying close
with moonlight faces
will never be enough.
We'll have to beat each other down
              by daylight
to understand why love is love
and why it's come to us in March
three months ahead of summer.

Venice

The birds waited
on the balcony
     this morning
for you to feed them
our leftover croissants.
Ignoring me you ignored
       the pigeons too
they chattered and complained
     all day long.
We came to Venice
so you might find the sun.
     Did you?

Was it in an alleyway
or Harry's Bar?
Did it move beneath
a gondolier's wide hat?
And did the sun
while eating up your skin
chew away the last of us
                    as well?

44

The sun
is a movable target.
It stayed with me
in St. Mark's Square
and followed you
            to Lido Beach.

I'm tired
of being next to you
just to engineer a tan.
I'd be the same man pale.

Tomorrow Cannes.
Another sun that
ends when I go home.
Then I'll be by myself
            in friendly shade.

I cannot excite you
with motor trips
or first-class
    airplane rides
        or voyages
where French cuisine abounds.
You live in worlds
      I'll never know
the stranger's smile
the journeyman's
approving glance
a night remembered once
that sends you
to the other side of bed
and keeps you there.

I tried by buying you
             a golden coin
a trip around the world
               and back
a passage to my secret self.
They were not enough.

I'll never be so rich
           or influential
as to excite you with myself.

I didn't run
my whole long life
toward this moment
to meet this time
to be told
by your indifferent eyes
that I am not as handsome
as I hoped I was. A mirror
could have told me that.

I came in hope of finding
a way to expand my own
                    reflection
to make it more
          than what it is.
If I must go away with less
fortify me with your smile.

The journey back is longer
than the forward run.

Noon

I watch you
slowly turning gold
beneath this out of season sun
and think how difficult
our life will be together
now that our independent lives
        are done.
I've made a rhyme
                without intention.
I only meant to put down
for some near
        or distant day to come
you turning brown all over
me turning over in my head
some doubts I've lately
                    come upon
that rack me for no reason.

Roll over on your back
and let the sun
      have this side
I'm off to gather
      sea shells
and some new composure
         if I can.

All of the bright young men
running out after the fun.
All of those bright young men
how pale they all seem
after chasing the sun.

—*Chasing the Sun*

April **for Bill Thompson**

The day's so warm
you can feel the sun.
What does it matter
what's done in the day
after the day is done?

—*Love Let Me Not Hunger*

April

I did not choose
an April birth
but I am ever grateful
that the month chose me.
Not because the earth
has taken for itself
that same coincidental
time
to start rebuilding,
but because
by all accounts
April is the only time
a man need not ask even God
for miracles
or transformations
they come unsolicited
and everywhere.

Tulips and the birth
                of grass
morning-glories
            in the morning
and lilacs all day long.
April holds a man so firm
that he could swear
the screech owl's singing
was a choir of blue jays
paid to serenade
            the neighborhood
like a touring medicine
            or minstrel band.

April is the tuning fork
for the summer months ahead.

Iowa from an Airplane

Above Iowa and looking down
the patchwork quilt of farms
unfolding through the oval window.
Now short green squares,
now broad gray triangles
and oblong stretches
of fresh-turned chocolate earth
that surveyors would find hard
                    to pace off.
Plots and pleats of land
orphaned from a quilting bee.

Though mid April
       grapples
with the middle earth
bare trees still
       stand bare.
Airports are the only
       eyesore
as silos dot
and red barns dash
   the land,
and God plays bridge
with unseen friends
and shows the world
       his hand.

Tractors
track the squares
and fences follow
every crooked line
they helped create,
though even fences
make no boundary lines
and Iowa in the eye
        seems full enough
to spill across the continent
if not across the world.

North Street Remembered

You'll have a phonograph
      a chef's hat
and a yellow suit
of your own choosing,
even if we have to
pay for them on time.
A canopy above the bed
that I can chin on.
A headboard
you can prop your head against
        and read.

You can write and polish words
while I sit quietly
       in some dark corner
         watching.

I'll teach you music
slowly and without pain
and you can show me
how to make a Quiche Lorraine.

I've never been up Beacon Hill,
      you can take me there.
Later in the summer
we'll go to that beach
       in Provincetown.
You can show me
where you started
writing out your poem.

Don't you see
I've got it all worked out
we'll follow every sun
        there is to follow.
We'll be equal in all things
you'll give me youth and you
I'll give you more of me
        than I yet know.
Each other we will give
        each other's other.

I'll lose weight, you'll see.
Before we leave for California
            Paris or wherever
we'll get it all together.

I never sleep so well
as when I'm sleeping
                next to you
or talk so much
as when I'm talking
        at your ear.
My hand
while touching
just your back
has touched the sky
as sure as God has groped
                the stars.

Ask my name
and it's now yours.
Demand my purpose
and you know it's you.
My needs are only
those wants you want.
And when I sleep this night
          or any after this,
though you be miles gone,
my head still rests
against your belly,
          moving down.
Or at your back
against your shoulders
moving not at all.

From a Letter

There were no seagulls
                    here today
warm winds have blown them
off to warmer sands.
To Spain or Greece
where there are rocks
and all the caves are
plentiful with clams.

Lying by the sea
I watch the *giogoli*
track the ladies
down the beach
thinking all the while
of Muir Woods redwood trees.

Green fields and sheep dogs,
red poppies seen
        from train windows.

You wouldn't like
        the beach today
the flags are all so tattered
the kites are all too few.
You'd be like me
wondering how I came to be here
not troubled but not happy.

God I hate this waste of time.
I should be chopping wood
or raking leaves
or home in bed
with all those tired dreams
I saved so carefully
for such days as these.

I could count the ceiling cracks
and feed the animals
their Crackerjacks.

Though I feel spent
let down and done,
trying to slow down
is not so easy
when your thoughts still
hang on yesterday.

Dodging pigeons in the square
while five-piece combos
grate my ears,
I'm restless all day long.

Apart I am
and much alone.

Did you feel the same
while riding home
        to California?
What were your thoughts and
secret wishes?

I'll tell you this—
you've earned the right
        to rest awhile
and occupy your time
with just the breakfast dishes.

I know what's happening to us
and I know why.
Outside myself I stand
looking back in abject amazement.

Fish Kites

We'll go to Tachikawa
    for the weekend.
As we slip by the fields
we'll see a hundred
      shades of green
run along the window
        of the train.

Boys' Day
and all the fish kites
will be flying
    from the rooftops.

Sink down into my lap
        and sleep.
Untroubled sleep
of those who know
that weekends only last
        two days
and have an address list
of long-forgotten names
to prove it.

Seventeen

Often I wonder
why we go on running.
There are
so few things pretty
left in life to see.

That is until tomorrow
when the crocus jumps up
back in California courtyards
and you become
my back rest
and my English bible.

Religious Experience

The horses would run
down the field
              and scatter.
Let out to pasture
they'd frisk like children
when the bell rings three
and school doors open.

At night
they'd all be back again,
coming to the barn
slow and single file.

When I didn't
chase the horses
        out to pasture
I'd go swimming
in the reservoir
off beyond the other side
                of town,
or sit above a certain pond
tossing pebbles at the water
just to see the circle form,
                widen
and then disappear.

One day coming home
I saw a farmer
pissing by the road.
His balls hung down
        below his hand
and looked so heavy
that I began to run
for no apparent reason.
I didn't stop
until I reached
the safety of my room.

Home again,
I pulled the shade
and got down
from the bureau
my Sunday School
          coloring book.
Having chewed
my brown crayola
just the day before,
I had no choice
          but to color
Jesus Christ's hair
          yellow.

I made his robe all green
and having no green left
to paint the shrubbery
outlined in black
against the stark
            white sky,
I left it as it was.
The same held true
for all the fishes
and the bread.

On Sunday next
my painting
was the best in class
and to this day
it's still the best one
that I ever colored.

That Sunday
and afterward as well
I started taking
a different road to home
bypassing my favored pond,
not even going near
          the reservoir.

Some time later
I learned to paint
        by numbers
but no one ever cared
as much for anything
I ever colored up
as that first
yellow headed Jesus Christ.

"Inspired," the Deacon said.
Even now it's hanging
        in the rectory.

April Man

An April evening
tangled in the river's tail
whining of itself
as the wind does
in the eaves
    of broken buildings.

Crickets—if they are crickets
sound like seagulls
    or the crackling fire
as every bit of life there is
is trapped above the river
                    or below.

I am not signaling
for May to come
nor tapping out
        a message
to the ears of June.
I'm held in place
and helpless,
like a given April night
the tail of some brown river
still holds onto.

I've brought you
nothing new
nor can I lead you
through tomorrow.
But if you travel back
to where I am
I'll let you stroke the tail
of my brown river
or wrap your naked limbs
around your battered brother
who has given in
but still remains
an April man.

Lilac Strain

There is a lilac strain
that runs the breadth of England
and yet no bloom is more maligned.

Superstition says that death
lurks within the house
that houses them.
And so the bower
        and the bush
are left untouched.

Their blooms are not plundered
and sold like daffodils.
Their branches never amputated
and trucked to town
like the early blooms
          of fruit trees.
Lilacs of all colors
stay protected from the vase
          and florist's visit—
for that one short month
that ends the Spring.

Passing Through Kansas

for Kelly in Manhattan, Kansas,
who hunted me out at the
Holiday Inn

The bright pink plumage
and white dogwood
threaten to cover
even abandoned birds' nests
that sprout from limbs
        like boils.

Nothing stops or checks
the progress of the willow.
It remains
for lilacs to cap off
the short lived spring
as hollyhock and Summer
open up again.

Write Me a Poem

Write me a poem.
Make me a song.
Tell me a story
I don't yet know.
Speak to me slowly
of fire and Friday
and tell me how nice it is
                 walking alone.

Not reassurance
but reason I need
For Spring's at the window
slowing the day down.

So write me a poem
using few words
my span of attention
is five lines, no more.

I'll catch the sun
and never give it back again.
I'll catch the sun
and keep it for my own.
And in a world
where no one understands
I'll take my outstretched hand
and offer it to anyone.

—*I'll Catch the Sun*

May   **for Bill & Judy Green**

Every day was Sunday
and every month was May
and every girl who came along
was sure to come your way.
How many years ago was that
ten, fifteen or more
when we lived at Sommerset
in that time before?

—Sommerset

Afternoon Shadows

The afternoon shadows
gather as the day goes home.
And now the in-between time
            before the night
      after the day.

Above the gray harbor
the city sits on white houses
waiting for the happenings
and all the boats are in.

A wind is coming up
and we'll be warmer
by ourselves at home.
I cannot look at you
reflected in the glass
behind this bar much longer.

I want to be
alone with you,
I want my thighs
to speak your name
so softly
only you can hear.

This place was made
for those who still
play hide-and-seek
we're home free.

To the Hills, Then

The sky
is the forehead
        of the morning
passing the sun
        along the day,
distributing the clouds
that move above us
and ride with us
        till nightfall.

And your eyes
are the bottom of the day
set on fire by words,
made to move by sighs
and the rustling
        of the trees.

We'll go to the hills then,
        take our time.
Climb until we find one
    closest to the sky.

I'll spread a blanket
        on the ground
and make a picnic
        of your body.
You'll face the sky
and count the clouds
and when the counting stops
I'll take you home again,
down a dozen hills
under a hundred skies.

I know the ground
is not yet green all over
        but trust me.
I'll find
the greenest hill of all
and your red dress
will be the single flower
that grows against the grass.

Me and the day
we care for you
without the rivalry
        of common lovers
and we'll be careful
        as the rain,
        gentle as the clouds.

May 24

Spring will chase us
through the summer
            into fall
and find us beached
upon some snowy shore
waiting for the spring
            to come again.

Then gingerly we'll go
          through jonquils
to seek out other summers.

Birthday to birthday,
       season to season,
every hour will be
     an anniversary
of the hour just past.

Afterward

The dandelion hasn't yet
been known to make a choice
between the pasture
         and the lawn
and love's as blind
to rank or right
as politicians are
to pulse beats.

Only desperation
cuts through
     everything.

Know that I'm
a desperate man
when in your arms—
and more so when away.
I wind my watch
when it needs no winding.
I puzzle harder puzzles
than my mind
          can comprehend.
By these simple acts
I manage for a time
to ward off facing
yet another
confrontation
with your absence.

How is it
that I've come to this
unable once again to fill up
even one more day alone?

Santa Monica Summer, 3

Chasing down the beach
            for grunion
        after midnight
        finding none
but stumbling over
            one another
on the way back home.
Part of another
Santa Monica summer
when all went well
        or did it?
Perspectives,
like horizons, change.

The facts are these,
I loved you
I meant to always be there
just as I meant
        to master algebra
somewhere along the line.
The line grew shorter
as the shadows all
grow longer now.

The need for algebra
began to fade
        as surely
as the need for you
grew stronger
and grows stronger still
now that you're away.

I did not intend
          to master you
but I wish I'd taken time
to learn more
          than your body.

That geography,
though dear enough,
was as incomplete
without the doorway
of your mind ajar
as a midnight hunt
               for grunion
several summers back
          in Santa Monica.

Hey Mr. Kelly,
ain't it a thrill
just to go runnin'
down some green hill,
rollin' on the green grass,
walkin' by the sea.
Caught in the sunshine,
Kelly and me.

—*Kelly and Me*

June **for Helen Brann**

In the summertime of days
a man is nothing more
than a tear in some old year
that was cast aside by God.

—*The Summertime of Days*

Mid-day

I watch the drudging ant
hike half across the yard
with some new-found stone
to help him and the others
finish off their pyramid.
And now another.
      And now another.
Crawling in a straight line
then zig-zag; jerking,
shaking like Chihuahuas.

Ants are not
        my favorite animals.
Or even on the list
of insects I like best.
And yet their industry,
not just a marvel,
is unbelievable
    compared to mine.

What have I done
              this season?
There is a book started
one long poem
not yet done
that I could count off
easier by the inch
than by the metered line.
A song I started
(death and dying
              once again)
not to be sung
even by its author.

At the season's end
a colony of ants
will have redesigned
finished and moved into
a brand new pyramid.

I'll have read
a few new books
some well loved old ones
                    over
and lost or never finished
what I set out to find.
Just now I can't remember
what that was.

I'm in the shade.
In the shade I'll stay,
   in the hammock
            swinging,
watching several lines
of worker ants,
hod and build and plaster
place each stone in place.

A sidewalk superintendent
sleepy eyed and slow
making sure that all goes well
beneath my still, unswinging
                hammock.

Toward Security

June is for juggling
getting rid of spring
and moving into
            summertime.
The beach is but a back rest
                waiting
to fold down into August.

In love,
we walk a tight-rope
as new brides dash
from Cincinnati churches
and rejects sling their rings
          into the Reno river.

When the sand starts singing
nobody else will hear but us.

Morning, Three

I rise up singing
from your belly,
like some glad keeper
of the palace swans
content to serve your navel
as an acolyte would serve
                his unseen god
and take your perspiration
                as communion.

Rolling now together
in our bedroom world
we'll map out elbows
and each other's backs.

There are some parts of you
    that have no highways.
Hairy forests cover
even well-worn paths
but every forest
has its own surprises
and the hiker
coming through the glade
can only marvel
            as Columbus would
at sailing past
the old world's edge.

Turning Point

The road turns here,
up ahead you see it
dissolving in the dust.

I would have you now
dissolving into me
suspended,
    held aloft
by my arms only.
Hanging on
but letting go.

The sky
is cloudless here
look above
and you can see it
blue on blue,
     bareheaded
and not breathing.

I would wish for you
        the same clear
        cloudless eye
seeking mine
straightforwardly and true
not breathing
and bareheaded
as I breathe my way
            through you.

The sun
is friendly here
look just left
and you can see it
warm but kindly so
and clearly caring.

I would ask of you
that you be ever warm
willing to be kind
not letting me forget
that kindness is the passport
                    and the proven way
for two to journey through
        a lifetime, each other,
            or a single summer's day.

This Yellow Sun

This yellow sun
is not of my choosing.

I am disposed toward
kinder things.
A bit of thunder
if it must be so
to jog my head
and start me waking
long before the coffee
blinks its eyes.

Camera

I stand just so.
Your camera winks me
        into permanence
acne scars
    tired eyes
wrinkles on my forehead
more naked
than I have ever been
(especially to one
I love so very much).

I used to be afraid
to look completely real
the sun was just my friend
            sometimes
when brown from sea and sky
made things all right—
always afraid to be
anything but young
and envying beauty
even on the face
            of strangers.

Is this what
growing up means
the reality of lighting
over public mirrors?
Or is my confidence in love
            so great
that I worry not
to let you see me
        at my worst?

Colombre d'Or

Colombre d'or
sits there blinking
like an owl in morning
amid Picasso paint
        and Calder tin.
The tourists waiting
for Anouk to come
are not unlike the me
of yesterday
        and other years.

I waited for the sun
I kept on waiting
for that thing
that some call morning
        to begin.

Night Thought

You've been
so long at the beach
you even taste like the sun
but the sun is much too warm
            even for love.

I mean—I want you
but night is only inches away
            and I can wait.

Meanwhile
watch the indolent butterfly
playing on the tall flower
in the yard
and think about
the sun's going down.
It always does you know.

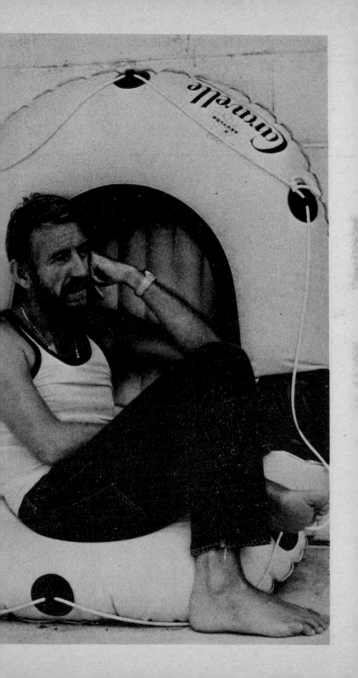

June 29

Who will keep
the brown days turning
        when we go?
It's hard to picture
all their moving parts
functioning without
        our hands to turn them.

The mechanics of *maybe*
        might not work
without an audience
of two or more,
that's why I never worry
        over rain.

No flood would think
to sweep our house away
for who'll be left
to watch the sunset
if we go?

June 30

There is no wrong side
    or right side.

No misery
in not being loved,
only in not loving.

I learned these truths
              myself
to tell them to you now,
as you go sailing
        through the sun
on your way toward life.

So I'll know
if I've done something
you'll remember
when I'm gone
walk me back
through summer moonlight
take me back
beyond the dawn.

—*Summer Moonlight*

July   **for Gerry Robinson**

Children playing on the sidewalk,
make me feel so all alone.
If I get through July,
sure as the heart is high.
When summer ends
I think I'll go back home.

　　　—*When Summer Ends*

July 4

I've come to know your body
        and your eyes
the way a child might memorize
      a favorite fairy tale.
Yet I need the reading
        once a night
the same as children do.

Don't leave out one dragon
or a single tree
that grows within the forest
that the Knight rides through.

So a child will tell you
of the story he loves best.

July 11

One by one the lights of the city
went out this morning
and the sun took over.

It moved on the mountains
like a young athlete
     doing push-ups.

It rose
stretched itself
and flexing its muscles
did backbends and push-ups
and showered in its own light.

On a hill this morning
God introduced me to the sun.

Now
with the sun shining in my eyes
I behold the pattern of the leaves
the variegated color of the hills
the beauty of marsh moss
and they are all pale
before you.

Extra Hour

Not by the sun's arithmetic
or my own
can I make the days
go fast enough.
Yet there are those
who beg God daily
for an extra hour.
I wish for them no solitude,
no time apart
          from what they love,
and let them
have their extra hour.

Sun

Warm is the day's end
multiplied
by all the warm days
            up ahead
and yet to come.
Sunshine is my solitary aim,
and my one ambition
is to capture
all the warmth I can
without a contract
            or condition.

The sun,
although predictable,
remains aloof
if not elusive.
It's not within my brain
to trap
and hold it
to myself—exclusive.
But as a seeker of the sun
I know without a doubt
warmness is the day's end
                    multiplied
by all the warm days
up ahead and yet to come.

Children of the Sun

Come home you children of the sun
enter doorways laughing, lingering,
staying for the space of this one
                    afternoon.
Going only when you're summoned
to supper and to sleep.
Coming yet another day
to climb my trees
    and trample down my roses.

Stretch out upon my grass
exercising your young limbs
in the sandlot game.
Come you children of the sun
save all your unsung songs for me.
Take liberties with my front yard.
Laugh at and with me.
Trust me as you trust each other.

That great ball of fire
stumbles now,
is sinking fast.
Expecting it to roll
            or stretch
through yet another day
is much too much to ask.
Now come you children
of the yellow sun,
begin your games
within the daylight left.

Land's End

Passers-by do still pass by
and short of keeping you
face down forever
I have to run the risk
when we go walking
of seeing wars flare up
on battlefields
       as yet unmarked.
If I must parade you
as the entry
in my midnight life
or show you to the sunlight
unmarked by my tattoo
         of ownership
I'll do so proudly
and without a chain.

I have in common with all men
a lump in swimming trunks
and most of us have freckles
on our shoulders.

Men are men.
The worst of us are lovely
           in the dark.
All of us are vulgar
when you've pulled aside
the final veil.

Some of us are gentle
after four o'clock.
Some of us are poor
in pride or pocket.
Some of us
    can make you rich
in plain or fancy rooms—
currency not being comfort
only given circumstance.

All of us,
and that's to each man,
need you more
than you need us,
we know that
and you know it too.

July's done,
it fell beneath
the knife of August sun
and out here where
the lonely pipers run
I walk beside
the oceanside,
as one.

—*Three*

August   **for Peter De Palma**

Jack Frost,
isn't it something
something to be seen
the long tall grass
waving in August
blessings in shades of green.

— *Blessings in Shades of Green*

August 5

Down the cliffs we go
to Marshall Beach
     stumbling
      smiling,
       single
        file.

With your skirts held
up above your knees
you call back images
of can-can dancers
tumbling through the doorway
of the Moulin Rouge.

Make the old men happy,
      little girl,
keep your skirts hiked high.
Give them more
     than summer sunshine
to fill their empty lives.

One day
twenty years from now
I might join
the beach-front line myself.
I hope the young girls
will be just as nice to me.

27 August, 1971

I know why
your belly's soft,
because so many men
have pressed against it
and into it.
So don't complain at my weight,
for when I come down
hard on you
it will only be
an act of loving
to wipe out all of those
indelible impressions left
by men mightier than me
and younger, yes—
but none who needed
your round belly more.

I shove my life
      deep into yours
until the melting
and the melding
brings us both so close
that cross or crowbar
will remain unable
to divide us.

The Adventures of Clark Kent

Your body lying easy
in the August day
is not a challenge
but an invitation.
Being lazy too
I leave it to the sun to ravage.
Night—
always more dependable
      than sunshine
has a way
of coming 'round on time
and I'm a patient man.

Don't think
I haven't noticed
those intrepid hikers
of the summer beach
who in the guise
of Sunshine Supermen
live out the tail ends
         of their afternoons
behind half-closed
         Venetian blinds
with what they've staked out
         on mid-mornings.

Notice though
the rope I've tied
about your ankle.
No Latin sun
can steal my mistress
for more than
just one afternoon.

Sunset

I wish nothing now
except to stay here spent
even as the day.

These arms the road's end
and your tired, tired face
already reaching into sleep
the climax of the climax.

Somewhere there are lovers
by blue rivers
going up steps hopeful
to a hundred foreign rooms.
I wish them well
for I have walked along my river
and found my room,
without the aid of any banister
I could in truth describe.

What Is It?

Cloud formations
on a given day
and wondering
if you've seen them too
are enough to make
a morning pass for me.

Was your day
filled with wanting
or the needle point
of knowing that I waited
and that I wait for you?

I did.
I do.

Swing safely home to me,
      come evening.
Make room for me
within your life
and I'll make room for you
within my arms.

If you don't know algebra
or Alice by the fire,
or even why some roses
fail to climb the wall,
ask the question of me.
Never be afraid to say,
What is it?

Cowboys, One

Brave
they straddle the animals,
hearts racing
    before the pistol sings
then leaping from the chute
man and animal as one
wedded groin to back.

One small moment in the air
and then the mud.

Hats retrieved
Levi's dusted
back to the bull pen
to wait the next event.

Sunday's choirboys
in cowboy hats.

Cowboys, Two

Huddled in the pits
below the grandstand
or lining at the telephone
to call home victories
they make a gentle picture.
Their billfolds
bulging just enough
to make another entrance fee.

Next week
    Omaha or Dallas.
San Antonio is yet to come.
And now the Cheyenne autumn
    like a golden thread
ties them
till the weekend's done.

Cowboys, Three

They wade through beer cans
piled ankle high in gutters—
the rodeo has moved
      down from the fairground
to the town
and every hotel door's ajar.
Better than the Mardi Gras.
The nights
are longer than Alaska now
until the main event begins
      another afternoon.

But after all the Main Event
is still be be a cowboy.
For ten minutes or ten years,
it's all the same.
You don't forget the Levi's
        hugging you all day
and Stetson hats
checked in passing windows
        cocked a certain way.

Some years later
when the bellies
flow over the belt loops
there's always
mental photographs.
Here the hero in midair.
Now the Dallas hotel room.
Now again the gaping tourists
licking off the Levi's
with their eyes.

Photographs of feeling
    mirrored in the mind.

Sure as the sun sets
and the world
rides on the wind
I'll be ridin' somewhere
with the cowboys again.

—*Gone with the Cowboys*

September

for Terry Jacks

There was a girl in Houston
Out where the hot wind blows
why I had to leave her
God Almighty knows
For she could take
the long hot summer
And cool it with a sigh
But words have no more wisdom
When it's time to say goodbye.

—*Love's Been Good to Me*

Indians

Comes now the summer
of unwinding.
The goldenrod riot
on the river bank
and all the frogs
sing new songs
as the world is emptied out
to suit the needs of man.

And our wants
grow stronger every day.
Thicket beds and flower rooms
       no longer do.
Sunshine is not enough
though it should be.

The Indian paintbrush
growing in the hills
reminds us that we can't
buy back the buffalo.

So we build another tower
and fence another red man off.
And with all the factories built
and all the black and red men
        safely fenced away
we'll die a total white
with nothing
but the gray of buildings
        for a shadow.

September 10

The year starts home.
Morning broke clear today
no fog . . . no rain
only a clear cold
September morning.

It's autumn all right
you can feel it
with the taste of summer
still in my mouth
my lungs breathe autumn.

The year goes back
from where it came
like a battered kite
being brought in
like a watch spring unwinding
like children to houses
when darkness comes.

Now night hovers
and madrigals begin again.

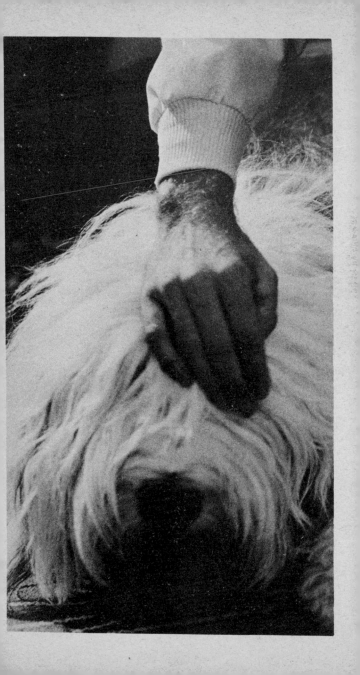

Patriot

Bare-bellied
in the bedroom
or coming from the bath
you look like every invitation
to every party I dreamed of
that never came.

I salute the sensibility
of your stomach
and pledge allegiance to it
as my only flag.

Planter's Moon

The moment
that the planter's moon
started down across your back
and promised me a harvest
great and good,
I knew that I had crossed
a different kind of field.
Greener than the ones
I'd trampled through before.

And if not safe
from all those eyes
lately gathered
        in a crowd,
curious and hoping
for the accident,
I knew it would be
            different.

I've kept my distance,
trying hard to keep the rules
and never violate the boundaries.
There were fences that I leapt
and some that I slid under,
even when I knew
I'd tear my pants.

Not equipped
with hook and ladder
I scaled walls
and burst through barricades
            and balustrades
as sure as any second-story man,
as certain as a centipede
all systems working.

I'd keep my arms spread wide.
I teetered on a tightrope,
    stretched between
your sometimes need for me
and tied securely
    by my always need for you.
Balancing,
    always balancing.
One foot before the other
down the rails and roads.

Three Finger Exercise

Hurry Sunday
or I'll die in Austria
a victim of Vienna's rain,
or worse I might decide
          to live
just to spite the spittle
even now coming down
          the window
keeping me inside.

Living in New York
ten years ago and more
I had a secret fear,
      a private worry
that I've never spoke about
even to a friend, till now.

The web of some umbrella
passing by unheeding
would gouge my eye
and leave me bent
half blind and
half a man
crouched
against
April's
dirty
wall.

I Have Loved You in So Many Ways

I have loved you
in so many ways
in crowds or all alone.
When you were sleeping
              beside me.
When you were away
and I imagined others
watching you in the street
or worse—
you in other people's arms.

I have seen the march
of beach birds and loved you.
I have lent myself
to summer sun and loved you.

And seeing naked trees
and raising my collar
        to the wind
and counting minutes
till chartered hours
            were there
I have loved you.

And the questions
        never asked.
The answers learned
        at love's expense.

I've promised myself.
I will not ask
where you have been tonight
I'll only say hello
            and hope.

With most of our summers behind
we hope that the winter is kind
as love leads us home through the fall
like the ivy that clings to the wall.

—The Ivy That Clings to the Wall

October   **for Gene Palumbo**

All our dandelion days are done
and so we'll run the fields no more
in search of wild roses
that grow out on the moor.

　　　—*Dandelion Days*

Octoberfest

On October mornings when it rains
I think back to Alamo and wonder
who picks up the apples
that fall into the puddles now
bobbing there like party favors.

Who swings his lunch pail
forward and back
going to that one-room school?
And does October come
to that brown barnyard
now that I'm no longer there
             to see it?

Some Distance

My credentials
jangling in my jeans
are I know
      not enough,
nor can my smile
do all the work
unless some magic
has happened in our eyes
           before.

I have come some distance
and I will go
    some distance more.
I would spend the interval
between the journey
      just completed
and the one to come
on the outside
looking into you
or on the inside
looking out beyond
the both of us.

October 2

follow me
and I will lead you
through the alleys
and down the darkened streets
               to home.

cross here
near the chalk marks
along the sidewalk
where children played
this afternoon.

lift your feet.
go quietly.
disturbing no one
on this sleeping street.

close your eyes
and the sight
of tall brick buildings
with dirty windows
will be gone.

stop a moment
and listen
to your own footsteps
echoing, resounding
through an asphalt alley.

One More Summer

Send me
one more summer
in the hills.
Pack it neatly,
arrange it so
that opened up
the whole of it
will spread around
a half a dozen
months or more.

Make it full
as any picnic basket
packed up tightly
with the things I love.

Every day
need not be warm.
Light rain should thread
could thread some days
          together.

Let me spend
those summer days
within my own country.
A citizen not of the world
　　　　　but here.

In my land
in my place
in or near
some town I've known
or lived in.

Perhaps—
but dare I ask?
Inside, beside
some face or arms
I've been inside before.

God of our fathers
if you're there
send another summer
please before I die.
The winter months
go on too long.

My great coat's
been on the rack
just inside the hall
near half a year now.

Too long. Too long
for one whose body's
       only healed
by summer's color.

White I am and ready
for another summer.

Hurry up
and in exchange
I'll spend the winter
just ahead and coming up
on my knees and praying.

We Thought Perhaps

We know the clocks
      are changing
but we've come prepared.
The three of us
have run all day
and all the season too.

You might expect us
to be tired. No.

It's just that
after thumbing
beach to beach
we thought perhaps
that somewhere
in our travels
going from the sand
or coming from the water
we might have accidently
          come by you.

A loss.
But totalling
this summer's gains
would not be fair.
And anyway
    how do you write down secrets
and make them
        not so secret any more?

The three of us
      (the dogs and me)
are maybe tired after all.

But we still hope to see you
      one more time
coming down the beach.

Looking Back

There is no single day
             or time
within the life
I've so far lived
that I'd have changed
             or altered.

Possibly there are some days
I could have missed
and never missed,
but I suspect that I could not
have come down to this place
             a different way.
As I suspect that being here
I don't as yet know where I am.

While walking in a lonely wood
I saw a big man fall a tree
his muscles bulging in the sun
he never said hello to me.

—*The Voyeur*

About the Author

ROD McKUEN was born in Oakland, California, and has traveled extensively throughout the world both as a concert artist and a writer. In less than five years six of his books of poetry have sold nearly nine million copies in hard cover, making him the best-selling and most widely read poet of all times. In addition he is the best-selling living author writing in any hard-cover medium today. His poetry is taught and studied in schools, colleges, universities and seminaries throughout the world, and the author spends a good deal of his time visiting and lecturing on campus.

Mr. McKuen is also the composer of more than 1,000 songs that have been translated into Spanish, French, Dutch, German, Russian, Czechoslovakian, Japanese, Chinese, Norwegian and Italian, among other languages. They account for the sale of more than one hundred fifty million records. His film music has twice been nominated for Motion Picture Academy Awards.

Rod McKuen's classical music, including symphonies, concertos, piano sonatas and his very popular "Adagio for Harp & Strings," is performed by leading orchestras in the United States and throughout Europe. In May of 1972,

The Royal Philharmonic Orchestra in London premiered his "Concerto #3 for Piano & Orchestra," and an orchestral suite, "The Plains of My Country." In October, 1973, The Louisville Orchestra premiered Mr. McKuen's latest commissioned work, "The City." In 1974, it was nominated for a Pulitzer Prize in music.

Before becoming a best-selling author and composer, Mr. McKuen worked as a laborer, radio disc jockey and newspaper columnist. Of his military service during and after the Korean War, the author says, "I was a private in the army who rose from that rank once only to descend rather swiftly."

The author makes his home in California in a rambling Spanish house which he shares with a menagerie of Old English sheep dogs and nine cats. He likes outdoor sports and driving.

Sources

"Rome Itself," "Afterward," "Land's End," "Sunset," "Planter's Moon" were first published in *Stanyan Street and Other Sorrows*.

"Twenty-Three," "From a Letter," "Seventeen," "Extra Hour," "Patriot" were first published in *Caught in the Quiet*.

"Pushing the Clouds Away," "Afternoon Shadows," "I Have Loved You in So Many Ways" were first published in *Listen to the Warm*.

"The Meaning of Gifts," "Toward Security," "The Adventures of Clark Kent," "We Thought Perhaps" were first published in *With Love*.

"Venice," "Fish Kites," "Morning Three," "Cowboys, One," "Cowboys, Two," "Cowboys, Three," Indians" were first published in *Lonesome Cities*.

"Iowa from an Airplane," "April Man," "Lilac Strain," "Santa Monica Summer, 3," "27 August, 1971" were first published in *And to Each Season*.

"To The Hills, Then," "May 24," "June 29," "June 30," "July 4," "August 5" were first published in *In Someone's Shadow*.

"Turning Point," "Religious Experience," "Children of the Sun" were first published in *Come to Me in Silence*.

"July 11," "September 10," "October 2" were first published in *And Autumn Came*.

"North Street Remembered" is from *Moment to Moment,* to be published by Simon and Schuster in September, 1974.

Certain other poems have appeared in periodicals and in the "Animal Concern/Rod McKuen Calendar," and a privately printed edition of *Moment to Moment.* Several of the poems have title changes and there are a number of works being published here for the first time.

Index to First Lines

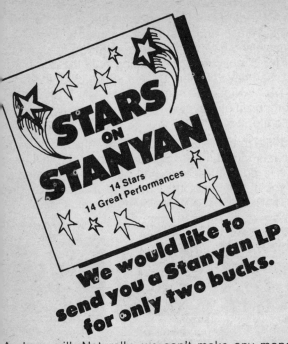

STARS ON STANYAN

14 Stars
14 Great Performances

We would like to send you a Stanyan LP for only two bucks.

And we will. Naturally, we can't make any money that way but we're gambling on the fact that once you play it, you'll want to hear some of the other recordings exclusive to STANYAN containing top performances by Rod McKuen, Alice Faye, Dinah Shore, Jo Stafford, Cleo Laine and many others. . . .

More than a dozen stars in a two–record salute to the Hollywood Canteen.

Nostalgia by the barrel load including performances by Vera Lynn, Noel Coward, Eartha Kitt, Carmen Miranda, Ramon Navarro and Fats Waller.

Great sound track and original-cast albums. Lush, beautiful music by great orchestras like Acker Bilk, The Stanyan Strings, The Violins of Versailles.

MUSIC FROM AROUND THE WORLD by Jacques Brel, Stanley Holloway, etc. . . . . Even a brand–new, never-before-released album of great performances by Judy Garland.

(Continued on other side)

STANYAN records are reasonably priced—since there is no middleman and this is not a record club (where you receive and have to pay for records you don't want). You order directly from the catalog only those records you yourself have chosen. Best of all, much of the profit from STANYAN goes to help ANIMAL CONCERN, a non-profit organization devoted to helping domestic animals and wild life.

If you'd like to order additional albums, the 6 below are $5.00 each, including postage and handling. We'll even throw in a complete catalog and other free nonsense. But if you'd rather not trust us, take a chance on the $2.00 STARS ON STANYAN album. You can't lose!

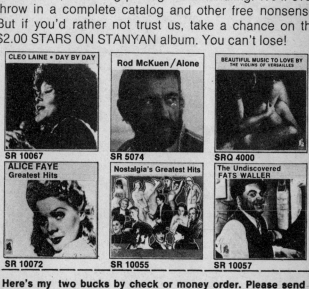